T0383867

CONNECT
TO YOUR
CALLING

CONNECT TO YOUR CALLING

T. D. JAKES

New York   Nashville

FaithWords
Hachette Book Group
1290 Avenue of the Americas, New York, NY 10104
faithwords.com
X.com/faithwords

First edition: June 2024

FaithWords is a division of Hachette Book Group, Inc. The FaithWords
name and logo are registered trademarks of Hachette Book Group, Inc.

The publisher is not responsible for websites (or their content) that are not
owned by the publisher.

The Hachette Speakers Bureau provides a wide range of authors for
speaking events. To find out more, go to hachettespeakersbureau.com or
email HachetteSpeakers@hbgusa.com.

FaithWords books may be purchased in bulk for business,
educational, or promotional use. For information, please contact
your local bookseller or the Hachette Book Group Special Markets
Department at special.markets@hbgusa.com.

Library of Congress Cataloging-in-Publication Data

Names: Jakes, T. D., author.
Title: Connect to your calling / T. D. Jakes.
Description: First edition. | New York : Faith Words, 2024.
Identifiers: LCCN 2023054969 | ISBN 9781546029359 (paper over board) |
    ISBN 9781546029342 (ebook)
Subjects: LCSH: Christian life. | Instinct. | Ability.
Classification: LCC BV4509.5 .J343 2024 | DDC 248.4—dc23/eng/20240131
LC record available at https://lccn.loc.gov/2023054969

ISBNs: 9781546029359 (hardcover), (ebook) 9781546029342

Printed in the United States of America

LSC-C

Printing 2, 2024

Contents

Introduction

"What's my calling?" "How do I find my purpose in life?" "Why am I so unfulfilled?"

These are powerful questions packed with poignant terms. They are questions that demand answers, yet those answers can only come from within. Each of us holds the key to our own calling, purpose, and sense of fulfillment.

What is that key? Instinct.

Scientists tell us that even our cells have instincts. Imagine my amazement when I spoke with physicians who revealed the way our physical cells operate. They say even our cells function based on what has been genetically programmed within them. Instinct is interwoven into the very fiber of our DNA.

We all begin as a single cell, the product of an egg and a sperm. They unite to form a zygote, the result of the fertilized egg, the single cell that will evolve from a

human forming to a human being. This new cell under-
goes a series of rapid divisions that produce a blastocyst,
the initial ball of new cells. The blastocyst then mul-
tiplies into many daughter cells. One expert describes
these cells as being "pluri-potential." In other words,
each of these cells has the potential to differentiate into
new cells of many different varieties. Some "daughter
cells" instinctively become skin cells, bone cells, spleen
cells, cardiac cells, or brain cells. The inherent imprint
of these cells activates them to become what they were
predestined to be.

This inherent sense of identity based on function is
truly astounding. Doctors explain that the cardiac cells
are "autorhythmic" cells. They actually vibrate and beat
together instinctively at the same tempo before they
ever unite with each other and function as the heart!
Even drummers in an orchestra need a conductor to set
a rhythm, but these cells instinctively catch the same
beat and have the same rhythm. They draw together
and beat together to the same rhythm.

Learning about these "cell instincts" made me think
of the old camp song taken from the Old Testament
book of Ezekiel. You know: the foot bone is connected
to the leg bone, and the leg bone is connected to the hip

bone, and so forth. Now, I'm not a doctor, and I'm sure not here to sing around a campfire. But what I want you to see is that the body develops from cells that find their rightful place because they know what they were made to do! These cells vibrate to the tempo of their purpose even before they're operating and performing their function.

So how about you: Are you in sync with your inner wisdom about your strengths, abilities, talents, and unique contribution to the world? Or is your life somehow off beat with your inner melody? Have you lost your rhythm because you have not found your place to define and activate your unique contribution? One of the great tragedies of life is not discovering the people, culture, and careers that are part of your tribe and moving to the same beat.

You may have experienced the discord that comes when those around you move to the beat of a drummer different from your own. Successful businesses, healthy relationships, and most collaborative endeavors require a syncopated alignment of roles, responsibilities, and rhythms. Entrepreneurs often need employees with a work ethic and flexibility similar to their own. It's frustrating when you have an urgent idea that requires execution at midnight and a team member who cannot be reached until the following day. It's not wrong to set boundaries and limits on work, but people need to be on the same page of music so the orchestra can play together. Similarly, romantic partners often discover they're out of step because one desires a waltz while the other's leading a tango.

Contentment comes when you find the people, places, and events in life you were created to impact. Most individuals who lead rich, productive lives do so because they allow their instincts to guide them to the intersection of the head and heart, the place where their deepest passions and sharpest skills align with destiny. They succeed instinctively because they each know their own tempo and recognize it in the individuals and institutions with whom they collaborate.

If you have ever felt misaligned, this book is for you. If you have lost the rhythm, the passion, or the thrill of living in alignment that you once glimpsed, then keep reading. As he did with the very cells that make up our bodies and the dry bones that were joined together for new life, God has given us deeper instincts to be attracted to those things that fit a higher and better purpose.

Never settle for less than God's best for your life.

Some people have the courage to move beyond the ordinary, from the methodically mediocre into the revolutionary realization of where they belong. You can have this sense of belonging only when you connect to your core calling. If you believe in calling, as I do, you understand it's more than the motivation to minister that clergy experience. The calling to creativity, the calling to teach, to give, to build, are all part of allowing your instinct to guide you to the "something more" that you suspect is out there.

Who can deny that some people move into their life's purpose with the skill of a child prodigy when he first touches a violin? They're aware of a compelling sense of attraction and engagement that cannot merely be taught but can only be caught. I've known musicians who played the piano from childhood, many without lessons. They just sat down at the keyboard and felt connected to it.

It's a sad thing to live your life without this deep-rooted sense of connection to your purpose. Like a lightbulb without a lamp, this kind of disconnect fosters dark and foreboding feelings in the soul. Whether you are the manager or the employee, the homemaker or the home builder, what matters most is that you have been awakened to your purpose and enlightened to the inner fulfillment that it affords.

Early in my life, I myself was haunted by feelings that I was created for more than I could access in my environment. The only reason I moved beyond the many potholes and pit stops I encountered is because of an instinctive allure pulling me toward something up ahead on the road that I had to find. I refused to stop and settle for less than the explosive exploration of what God had placed within me!

There is no secret formula for learning to listen to your instincts and connect with your calling. These pages before you merely offer my sparks toward kindling the blaze of your own incandescent, instinctive alignment, the deeper and fuller life you were created to attain. So as we journey together, let's remove the smoke and mirrors and ask the questions at the heart of our truest self. If we seek meaning in our motives, perhaps the answer will be not the voice of God shouting at us from the heavens but the whisper of our God-given instincts deep within.

You see, Scripture tells us that out of the heart flow

the issues of life (Prov. 4:23). The heart can't read. It can't draw and it surely can't drive. But if we will listen to its drumbeat, if we have the courage to be wooed by its wisdom, then we will find our answer. We could spend the rest of our lives in a rhythm so in sync that the melodious sounds we make transform all areas of our lives into an integrated, harmonic symphony of satisfaction.

As we grow and go forward, our master Creator may be wooing you instinctively into a place where your intellect can flourish and your heart can rest. If cells move until they connect and form the highly complicated and efficient beings we call humans, then maybe we need to put our ears to the heart of the matter and catch the beat.

If these words resonate with you and reverberate with what you know to be true, then it's time to decode your own instincts, increase your areas of advancement, and illuminate the dark corners of disappointment at the edges of your life. It's time to connect with your calling. I truly believe that following your instincts will transform your workplace, liberate your career, and enhance your relationships.

Make no mistake: these pages can only offer you clues to stimulate your own process of discovery. The answers you seek are already inside you. So if you're ready to unlock the confines of where you are to discover the freedom of where you were meant to be, then let's get started. Remember, your instinct is the key!

CHAPTER 1

A Safari Secret

Our Creator designed everything he made to have a purpose. Yet most of us live our lives wondering what our purpose is. Worse still, there's an aching in our hearts as we sense that there has to be more in life, something beyond the monotonous compliance with convenient opportunities to which most of us have lived our lives. I encounter so many people who dread going to work—not because they are lazy but because they are unfulfilled.

Without understanding the guidance that our innate God-given instincts provide us, we simply adjust to the urgency of circumstances, all the while sensing deep within that we were created for so much more. Yet the uncertainty or fear of pursuing this inner sense keeps us contained in the contrived cage of the ordinary. Simply put, we've never learned to rely on our instincts.

But regardless of where we are in life, it's not too late to align our lives with the inner wisdom of who we really are and what we were made to do. God, the master designer, has equipped us with a fundamental instinct that draws us to our divine purpose. This sense of potential being realized is more fulfilling than any paycheck. It is the feeling of fitting in, like a piece in a puzzle, to form a greater picture than what we may be doing right now. It is the innate satisfaction that comes from giving the gifts that you and you alone can contribute to the world.

How do instincts help us connect to our calling and find true purpose in life?

First, instincts provide us with information that has been synthesized through the filter of who we really are and our truest goals in life. Facts, data, information, and knowledge provide nourishment and stimulation for this capacity within us. Our powers of observation and of experience are stored here. Our creativity, resilience, and resourcefulness also abide within our instincts. Fused together, the basic instinct in each of us compels us toward the unique fulfillment that is ours alone.

Second, please understand that the kind of instinct we're talking about here is not an uncontrollable urge, self-indulgent desire, arbitrary impulse, or compulsion. Instinct may seem similar to these other aspects of our humanity at times, but ultimately our instincts include an acute sense of timing along with an awareness of self and others that transcends selfish lusts and addictive desires. In other words, our instincts are not motivated by immediate gratification, personal gain at the expense of exploitation, or the pursuit of satisfaction untethered from conscience.

Third, since we are made in the image of our Creator, I'm convinced that our instincts bear the imprint of the divine. As human beings, we not only possess the instinct for survival, just as any other living creature does, but we also have instincts for purpose, fulfillment, and dominion. God made us to reflect his creativity, resourcefulness, and imagination. He wants us to see beyond the literal, above the bottom line, and beneath the surface of appearances.

There is indeed a great deal of difference between a job and a career, a place of employment and a rendezvous with destiny. Finding the thing you were created to do can be a dubious task, highlighted by the fact that we generally don't have time to do the soul-searching required to find the hidden clues to unlock our fullest and best potential. Instead, we fill out an application, gain a reasonably good-paying job, and go to work for someone who found the thing they were created to do!

This inward urging or prompting is far too often underutilized, and consequently so many people feel stuck at a certain stage even as they long to be more productive. Beyond pursuing the direction of their instincts, as you may have done at times, the question remains: Have you maximized your findings or only stored the data and acquiesced to the mundane routine of fitting in with what has already been done?

Isn't it about time you activated what you've been given inside you?

Water for Elephants

My own life-changing encounter with the power of instinct in action occurred on a safari in South Africa. Yes, the kid who grew up playing in creek beds behind his house now felt an even keener thrill as I found myself lurching over open terrain in a Jeep! In fact, there was no way I could ever have imagined what a truly life-transforming event this safari would become, catapulting me into the "Aha!" moment that inspired this book. I wasn't there to stalk big game but to hunt for insight into this new world of roaring lions, zealous zebras, and the creatures that have always, for some unknown reason, fascinated me: elephants!

The first morning I was up before the sun and enjoyed a delicious pancake breakfast on the lanai before donning my newly acquired khaki safari suit. We climbed into the Jeep and met our guide. He was a distinguished gentleman who was incredibly knowledgeable, and I listened intently as he unloaded priceless information about the habitat, eating and mating habits, and so much more concerning the beasts that inhabited the wild.

Honestly, it all felt a little surreal. Considering my background, I marveled at this "If my mother could see me now" moment. Without a doubt, we were entering a world that couldn't be more different from where I grew up. The African wilderness has unspoken rules and regimens that the zoologist guide shared with us as

I oriented myself in this new environment so foreign to my background and previous points of reference. There were no street signs, traffic lights, or road manuals, just the voice of the zoologist guiding us along the way.

We saw gazelles leaping in the air like grease spattering in a cast-iron skillet at a fish fry. They skipped and lunged forward so fast that my camera palpitated in cardiac arrest while I snapped away as fast as I could. We spied on lions with their cubs, resting in the shade. Later we watched zebras move like painted horses loosed from a carousel. So much beauty, energy, and primal instinct came alive before us, more vivid and startling than any IMAX, HD, or 3D film could ever hope to capture.

As the sun hovered above the horizon like a scarlet ember, we looked for a place to make camp. It had been a good day, an unforgettable day. My only disappointment, which I kept to myself, was that we had not seen any elephants. The powerful pachyderms had eluded us all day, and as the sunset melted into twilight, I assumed that we had missed our chance. But then our zoologist guide casually mentioned that he looked forward to showing us the elephants tonight.

Had I heard him right? He planned to be out here at night! And for us to be with him? I swallowed hard and acted brave as we persevered deeper and deeper into the entrails of a world completely new and now even more foreboding, draped in shadows. Now, there were certainly a lot of animals I did not want to encounter in the dark of the African wilderness. And elephants remained high on that list. Nonetheless, as we continued bouncing along the dimly lit path that was our road, it was clear that our guide intended to save the biggest, if not the baddest and best, for last.

Soon our driver stopped the Jeep, and a man draped in loose native garb seemed to appear out of nowhere alongside us. Our guide told us that he was a Zulu and he would be assisting us this evening. I couldn't help but remember my history classes from junior high about Shaka Zulu the warrior, and I imagined that he might have looked like this stoic, dark-skinned man who proceeded to perch on the edge of our Jeep in a makeshift chair that looked as though it had been welded onto the hood to accommodate his small but muscular frame.

Apparently, he knew where to find the elephants. But based on his silent, impassive demeanor, I wasn't so sure. We hadn't seen one all day. If our zealous zoologist couldn't locate them, how was our new addition going to find them?

As our journey continued, the zoologist began spouting a fountain of scientific information about the area. However, I noticed the Zulu seemed unimpressed by the intellectual prowess of the other man, who continued to lecture with impressive factual data about our surroundings. The ancient-looking warrior remained silent as we careened deeper into the bush, jostled by bump after bump, until suddenly he opened his mouth and proclaimed, "The elephant is ova dere!"

Seated between a zoologist and a Zulu, between intellect and instinct, I saw something more startling than I had seen all day. I realized that intellect can explain an elephant, but only instinct can find one! The zoologist had used hundreds if not thousands of words to describe the environment where we might find elephants, along with their eating habits, mating patterns, and fighting skills. And yet the Zulu waited quietly, listening to something even more powerful than his counterpart's knowledge, and uttered five simple words: "The elephant is ova dere!"

Moments later, his instinctive exhortation proved

true. Proceeding in the direction the Zulu was pointing, our driver careened over rocky roads into a clearing by a small lake. There, a herd of elephants lounged and frolicked like guests beside the pool at the Ritz. Throwing water over their heads with their long trunks, they ignored their new spectators and continued cavorting.

I was speechless. Such power and might. Such enormous grace and agility on such a gigantic scale. We took picture after picture and had an incredible time, but I couldn't get out of my mind that God had brought me all the way to South Africa to show me something. Through this simple encounter, he revealed a profound metaphor on how to position my life and career for the future.

You see, it was there that I realized that I must not only surround myself with talented, well-informed people in order to prepare for the future. I must also include those individuals gifted with what the Zulu had afforded us. He reminded me that most things are not captured or conveyed by intellect alone. In fact, intellect without instinct can only explain and explicate but not execute. Only instinct can successfully find what intellect explains.

This is the one thing that university degrees and

on-the-job experience cannot instill in you. Your professors and bosses can invest countless hours exposing you to critical information and inspire you with empirical historical data that will be invaluable as you trek through life. But the gift they cannot give you is the instinct to know when to do what only you can do and where to do it!

That gift is necessary when we strive to pursue our purpose and connect with our calling.

In order to harness your intentions with your actions, you must rely on instincts. Every visionary learns that they must be well-informed and well equipped to accomplish their targeted achievements. But they must also be in touch with their instincts in order to use their experience, education, and equipment to fulfill their expectations. Instincts can help connect the dots between where you're trying to go and how you will get there.

From Zoologist to Zulu

The lessons of South Africa stayed with me.

I realized that my father certainly knew this truth as he built his one-mop, one-bucket janitorial business into a fifty-two-employee company. Dad had instincts to increase. Great preachers experience this urge as they unload a biblical text. Gifted leaders recognize that knowledge and talent are not enough as they navigate through crucial decisions. Movie stars know the secret to being more than just an actor. Instincts separate the mighty from the mediocre!

How about you? Do you have the instincts to know when you are on to something or when you are just going for a ride? Do you trust your instincts when making a business deal or hiring a new employee? If not, you may attain a modicum of success, but you will never fulfill your maximum potential until you advance from being a zoologist to becoming a Zulu!

This insight changed my prayer life, altered my interview process, revised the way I evaluated effective friendships, and ultimately thrust my vision forward from the ordinary to the extraordinary. All of my life I had thought that some people had it and some people didn't. But I didn't really have a word to describe what my eyes had witnessed. Now I can tell you what "it" was, that crucial difference that makes magic out of the mundane.

Thanks to an encounter at the tip of a continent

thousands of miles from my home, I now had a term for the nebulous criteria for successful living. It wasn't just talent. It wasn't just intellect.

I had found the secret of champions. As I went back through all the people I had met in my life like a reel-to-reel tape stuck on rewind, suddenly it all made sense. From concert stages to corporate lunches, from church revivals to courtroom closing statements, the one thing each encounter had in common: instincts!

So if you are going after the big game of an idea, remember that elephant tracking requires instincts you may not have had to use when chasing rabbit ideas! It isn't just intellect or even understanding. It isn't just giftedness and opportunity. It is the gift of activated instincts. Where do they come from? How can we sharpen them? How can we utilize what our creative Creator has invested in our deepest parts? Yes, I said *in*vested in all of us—to adapt, to transform, to create, and to sense moments of significance or danger. Moments to be wary and moments to be warring. When to cringe and when to capture. How to craft and not to crash.

It is the law of instincts that determines how we manage the moment, move into position and adapt, resourcefully create, and strategically forge ahead without fear. The common denominator of instincts wins presidential elections, makes comedians successful, causes architects to build timeless monuments, and elevates engineers to artists.

Living by instinct elevates your ability to know where you're going and how to get there. It can help you know when to slow down and step back and when to accelerate and step up. And it can guide you to what you're ultimately looking for—whether that's the elephant in the room or the elephant ova dere!

CHAPTER 2

A New Terrain

How do we activate our instincts in a way that guides us toward our calling? I'm convinced everything starts with exposure. You cannot be what you do not see. It isn't that exposure gives us instincts; it's that exposure awakens instincts and stops us from ignoring what we know to be true within us. Most people adapt to their environment more quickly than they should. They adjust themselves to the situation rather than adjusting their situation to the dreams they have inside.

You'd be surprised to find that you have accepted and adapted to being much less than what you're capable of becoming. It's alarming that people seek to fit in without considering the power they have to cultivate the gifts they've been given. You may even be mystified as to why you aren't further along in life. You have checked off all the boxes on the recipe for success and yet find yourself falling short. Isn't it time for you to understand what you've been given and how to sift the stirrings within so that your survival instincts can surface?

As the Zulu taught me, you must combine all your ingredients with the inner wisdom that God has given you if you expect to thrive. My prayer is that you will experience the same kind of revelation that struck me while sitting in a Jeep in South Africa as a wizened tribesman proclaimed, "The elephant is ova dere!"

Identify Your Identity

I have a set of twin boys—well, I say "boys," but my sons are actually grown men now. And while they are fraternal twins, not identical, with the same mother and father, they couldn't be any more different. When they were still in the crib, I noticed each had a distinct personality that continued to evolve and solidify as they developed. One is personable and artsy; the other is quiet and independent. One is nurturing and compassionate; the other is responsible and diligent. One is spontaneous and social; the other is methodical and private.

I'm certainly not a licensed clinical psychologist trained in early childhood development. I'm just a father who started out peeking over their cribs. While my wife and I never intentionally tried to make them conform to the same personality type, I'm sure we assumed that they were more similar in temperament than they actually were. We probably dressed them alike when they were too young to protest and worked to make sure each got the same attention. But clearly they were not alike!

And as they grew through puberty into young adulthood, I continued to ponder how two people so closely intertwined in such a small place as the womb, raised in the same house, and parented in identical environments could gravitate to such different clothing, diverse types of friends, and separate courses of life.

In observing them as adult men, I remain fascinated to watch them unpack their inventory of uniqueness and become acquainted with the substance of their individuality as they pursue the fulfillment of their divine potential. It's been an often raucous adventure as they've explored and discovered their own uniqueness, for each brings a distinctly remarkable thought pattern and skill set to problem solving.

Perhaps the primary reason for their successful development as independent, distinct individuals pursuing their purpose is their commitment to discovering the power of their own talents, abilities, and proclivities. They clearly are not clones of each other, and they haven't simply become the opposite reaction of each other.

Because they're twins, though, they probably faced the challenge of self-discovery sooner and more deliberately than most of us. And yet their accelerated journey is the same one we're all making: to know who we are created to be, to know why we're here on this earth, and to live out the pursuit of our divine destiny.

In other words, to connect with our calling!

Like my twins, many of us share the same variables for success as others around us, and yet we each fail to discover our distinct, personalized combination to unlock that success. Have you ever wondered why people with less talent, fewer resources, and more obstacles than you pass you by? Have you ever attempted to follow a formula or check off five "easy" steps to fulfillment only to become frustrated and feel like you're the exception? Too often, we imitate others and conform to popular standards but fail to tap into our most powerful, most precious resource: our own uniqueness.

Obviously, my twin sons share numerous similarities, the result of both genetic factors and environmental influences. But the fact remains that each of them was divinely designed as a one-of-a-kind, inimitable reflection of his Creator—not of his twin or even his parents.

As they matured, my twin sons naturally noticed the ways in which they differed from each other but, more important, they relished, cultivated, and celebrated these differences. As I mentioned before, they were more self-aware and more determined at an earlier age to discover their own personal abilities, interests, and passions. As much as they loved each other and enjoyed being twins, they nonetheless didn't want to be a duplicate of someone else, certainly not each other. Like each one of us, each wanted to know the fingerprint of his own personality. They were blessed to have both the motivation and the freedom to explore their inner resources.

Growing up, many of us aren't encouraged to

identify our individuality; in fact, we were likely told both in word and by example to conform, to fit in, to not stand out. Whether it was overtly expressed or covertly implied, the message we got was to accept the status quo and not make waves. This may have been our parents' attempt to make life run more smoothly or even to protect us from the scrutiny and often cruel mockery that comes from standing out in a crowd.

And yet, most of us knew at an early age that we were not like everyone else, let alone who others wanted us to be. It might have been our desire to stay indoors and get lost in the adventures of the Hardy Boys or Harry Potter instead of playing pickup basketball in the park.

From my experience and observations, our true identity rarely enjoys the freedom to emerge without first enduring conformity, social modification, or outright suppression. Peer pressure as well as parental expectations and the demands of our circumstances all exert various amounts of force on who we really are. Our instincts may have even guided us to hide parts of ourselves in order to keep them alive when we were younger. We instinctively knew that we could not express our creativity, unleash our imagination, or announce our dreams without them being injured by the ridicule, rejection, or retaliation of others.

As adults, however, we now have the power to liberate ourselves. We need no one else's permission to empower the God-given essence of our identity! Whether we think we have the time, money, or other resources needed to uncover who we really are, it's vitally important that we discover our core and allow it to grow, develop, and flourish.

You see, it's not about whether you can afford therapy or complete your education or attend that self-improvement seminar. And it's not about becoming self-absorbed, babying your inner child, or excusing self-indulgence. It's simply about whether you have the courage to look within yourself and embrace all that you find there!

Decode Your Design

Once you're ready to activate your instinct for success, you must actively seek elements of excellence that inspire you. Are you aware of what truly fascinates you? What appeals to your heart and ignites something deep inside you? The news articles that arrest your attention, the topics that tantalize your thought process, the curiosity that compels your unquenchable questions? These are the areas where you can begin to energize your instincts of identity.

The decoding process does not require a battery of aptitude tests, personality panels, or psychoanalysis. It simply requires you to become a student of yourself. Right now, go and see what you have bookmarked as "favorites" on your computer. Look at the images you've collected on Pinterest. What do they all have in common? Whose Twitter feeds have you been compelled to save and return to again and again? What magazines do you always pick up while waiting in the dentist's office? Which blogs magnetically pull you back to ponder another's observations and affinities?

Please keep in mind that you must be honest with yourself here. Cut through the books on your bedside table that you're supposed to read or the Snapchat exchanges you feel obligated to return. Others may not know about these interests and excursions in your life, but you know they are there. Your dream to run a bed-and-breakfast. Your curiosity about how to create a new investment portfolio. Your guilty pleasure of reading romance novels. Your ability to sew a jacket that looks like something off the rack.

These are the clues that are all around you, my friend! Use your instincts to guide you to what you love but may not have allowed yourself to admit. Dredge up your favorite memories of childhood and what gave you pleasure. Was it building new, never-before-seen structures with Lego? Creating stories about your friends set on another planet? Caring for your pets with the love and attention of a new parent? Whatever once had the power to float your boat can still rock your world!

It may feel silly or childish at first, embarrassing to admit, or crazy to consider. But search through the archaeology of your own ambition. Don't disregard any attraction, interest, passion, or proclivity as being too "out there" to examine and extract information from. You never know what you might discover by thinking outside the box that culture, conformity, and critics have tried to impose on your ideas.

Once you have a decent list of these personal preferences and uniquely special variables, look for patterns, similarities, and common denominators. Group them according to how they move you, speak to you, motivate you, and stimulate you. What sparks your creative impulse? Who motivates you as a role model? Where do you feel most alive?

Nothing is off-limits as you explore. You are the most fascinating person you will ever know! So don't cover up, deny, suppress, or pretend otherwise. Allow the true you to come out, the softer side, the edgier side, the creative side, the more organized side, the driven side, the liberated side, the "Who cares what people think?" side, and the "This makes me feel alive!" side. This is the soil where you will discover seeds planted long ago, waiting to burst through the surface of your consciousness and bear fruit. This is the galaxy of stars that can illuminate your journey through whatever darkness you may encounter. This is the area that can give you the satisfaction of knowing that you and you alone are doing what only you can do.

If this excavation process intrigues you, then I invite you to spend some time uncovering your greatest vital resources. I merely provide these questions and suggestions here as catalysts for this lifelong learning process.

CHAPTER 3

First Steps

So often we look to others for inspiration, approval, or affirmation of what we should do and how we should do it. But you will never achieve the fulfillment of your vision this way. My friend, you are the single most effective source for outwardly manifesting all the visions, inventions, books, or businesses that are naturally part of your gifting. This explains why being copied is never an issue, since true creativity can never be synthesized.

You were created to bring something to this earth that has never crystallized over the eons. I don't know what that is for you, and you may not have fully discovered it yet, but if you live and lead by your instincts, your rare and precious gift—one-of-a-kind—will emerge!

So stop manufacturing synthetic ideas or letting others pull your strings, and you won't have to fight off the competition. Put your seal, your scent, your essence, your DNA, on what you produce, and it will forever have that uniqueness. Stop copying and start discovering what is intrinsically within you.

Several years ago I founded a festival called Mega-Fest, an amalgamation of diverse interests of mine intersecting in one setting. My propensity for business themes and personal health merged with my passion for faith and spirituality. The very first year, over a hundred thousand people came from all walks of life to attend the event. Multiple countries and cultures were represented, and it was an unprecedented success.

However, the indelible moment of satisfaction that still lingers with me occurred the night before Mega-Fest opened, as I marveled at how my vision had come to life. Without formal training or much experience, my team and I received international kudos for organizing such a massive undertaking with only a few minor glitches. More important, we were able to motivate, inspire, entertain, and invigorate a diverse body of people, encouraging and challenging them to enjoy the contentment that comes from living in the bull's-eye of their life's God-given goals.

Through that first MegaFest, I gained an even greater appreciation for what it means to actualize your instincts and pursue purpose.

Let's talk about a first step in that process. Actually, let's talk about three first steps—three specific ways you can use instincts to launch this journey of discovering your destiny.

Instinct Takes Inventory

Before you build a team, open a ministry, start a business, launch a concept, or develop a plan, you must begin to inventory what's on the inside of you. There is some powerful potion that's inherent in people who produce outwardly what is theirs. No, I didn't ask you what you could afford or what you studied at the university or seminary. I'm merely asking you to understand that instincts begin with inclinations that you may not have acted upon but should at least explore.

Just as it's possible to have never been exposed to

a pool but be gifted as a swimmer, you may not have discovered your arena of greatness yet. Most creative, instinctive people ignite their passion by being exposed—sometimes even in the middle of their lives—to new ideas, other people, unusual positions, and unknown careers that they may not have encountered in their upbringing or normal environment. And yet they find themselves innately drawn to the beauty of a work of art, the brilliance of a new app, or the insight of fresh voices.

Scripture tells us that deep calls out to deep, and I'm convinced that those people, places, and perspectives that resonate with us often do so because of a shared, kindred quality. When something you encounter resonates with you, pay attention. Become a student of your deepest passions and most persistent curiosities. Notice the people you admire and feel drawn to emulate. We instinctively recognize members of our own tribe no matter how different they may look!

Just because the goose lays eggs on land doesn't negate the fact that her offspring are drawn to the water. And the so-called ugly duckling often realizes it is really a swan in disguise! Can you go past where you started to discover what you could be? Listen to your instincts and you will find your power.

Our greatest power doesn't always emerge from our experiences, not even from our most intense ones. There's incredible hidden treasure locked up in your instincts that may not always show on your résumé. If you can spend some time with yourself, you may be on the verge of the most powerful part of your life, discovering what's inside that your instincts want to express outside.

Think about what you gravitate toward when given time to relax and recharge. Are you always watching cooking shows on the Food Network, tinkering with recipes to make them your own? Maybe you're exploring new apps, thinking about the ones you wish existed that you can't find. Do you find yourself perusing history books and travel brochures about a foreign land or culture that captivates you? Are you drawn to the latest leadership training course that's coming to town?

Paying attention to what nourishes and stimulates your heart, soul, and imagination leads to listening to your instincts. In turn, listening to your instincts jumpstarts the process of creating the fabric of your destiny.

Like a designer sewing a garment, you take the vision within you and bring it to life in a suit to be worn for your next season of life. You are instinctively best at inventing what is in your inventory!

Instinct Adapts

When you follow your instincts and transform your vision into reality, you will discover that accidents, mistakes, and conflicts become creative material. Rarely do you have everything you think you need in order to succeed. Living by instinct allows you to adapt to change and grow stronger. Instinct often processes, learns, and accepts change before we do. Once our emotions, intentions, and abilities catch up, we move forward, one step closer to seeing our dreams realized.

This idea began as a hypothesis in me and was affirmed as I deepened my research and discovered some compelling studies on the subjects of creativity and innovation. I've always believed that we are an extremely adaptable species. Our country's development reveals this adaptability in our founders' tenacious pursuit of creating a powerful new nation even amid the uncharted wilderness of a brand-new frontier—or at least it was new to them.

My ancestors modeled the concept of instinctive adaptability when they were snatched from their motherland and had to adapt to a world that was not only brutal but totally unfamiliar: a new language, a new faith, new foods, new customs, and new rules of engagement. I don't know how they survived such a hostile takeover of their heritage and culture. But they survived and adapted and endured.

I can see it in my own life as I have survived many changes of my worldview, catastrophic economic and health challenges, losses, disappointments, and moments of intense anguish. I have survived the magnanimous moments of intense accomplishments that catapulted me into strange new arenas for which I had no training or preparation. Trust me, both success and struggle are different kinds of trauma.

But at my core I have always been a survivor. And though I may react to the trauma emotionally, shed private tears, have a meltdown away from people, or enjoy a complete *One Flew Over the Cuckoo's Nest* episode, when I'm finished expressing emotion, I keep on keeping on. When I finish my rant, tantrum, or moment of grief, I move into the instinctive survival mode that has empowered humans to endure plights and pleasures of all kinds. Change is often as painful for me to endure as it is for anyone else, but I have learned to take the bitter with the sweet and keep moving forward.

Why? Because doing so is critical to my calling.

Everything I have been able to accomplish and most of the exceptional accomplishments of others I've witnessed resulted from something that's hardwired into our cores. Some download better than others, but I believe all of us have more talents stocked in our inventory than life's demands require from us. It could be that oppositions and opportunities alike challenge us to draw from our inventory that which we might've been oblivious to otherwise. Think of how many things you had in you that required a challenge or a change to help you discover, utilize, and embrace.

Instinct Inspires

As I've researched adaptability, I've discovered some critical information on what I see as a pattern. Science teaches us that the role of instincts in determining the behavior of animals varies from species to species. It appears that the more complex the neural system of the animal, the less that species is inclined to rely on instincts.

Generally, from a biological perspective, the greater the role of the cerebral cortex—which draws on sociological constructs for learning—the less instinctive the creature becomes. Both its defenses and needs are accomplished by its supreme ability to deduce and decide. It doesn't have to rely on instincts because of its biological neural system. It isn't that the instincts aren't there. They are simply not the primary resource for rescue and resiliency.

With this in mind, I wonder if this in fact describes what has happened with us as we react to life in the twenty-first century. Some people live on and lead from their instincts, but most of us rely on intellect, social conditioning, and logic. Myriad voices scream at us daily from every source imaginable, and, sadly, we become deafened to the whispers of our own instincts.

Perhaps, in a perfect world, working with someone fully engaged with both facts and feelings would be a dream. They would regard facts but not ignore feelings. They could censor data meticulously but also have creative instincts capable of overriding what may seem logical on paper but impractical in execution.

This is the opiate of advancement. It liberates the soul to escape the obvious when need be and break beyond the historical orthodoxy of the previously held ideology. Through this union of timely information and the creative impulse of the instinct, we forge ahead into new excursions of ideas!

Yes, we all have instincts, intuition, and internal discernment. However, some never allow the activation of what is on the inside. Some people maintain that our intellects should eclipse our instincts. They have even suggested that the more cerebral we are, the less we benefit from relying on instincts. Nothing could be further from the truth.

Sometimes we've deadened the nerve endings of our instincts by indulging in the luxury of deciding by the numbers and living in the books instead of creating in the crosshairs of crisis. We don't use what we think we don't need. And as long as what we have been taught provides for us, why would we look deeper to unleash the many other gifts that are intrinsically stocked within all of us?

Recently I toured Nike headquarters, and one of the

displays had a tennis shoe stuck in a waffle iron. The company's cofounder, Phil Knight, had partnered with a guy named Bill Bowerman, and they each contributed $500 to start the company! In the early years of the company, Bowerman was inspired by a waffle iron to develop a sole for better running, with less weight and more traction. Who could've imagined that a waffle iron–inspired running shoe would become an iconic international brand? How's that for thinking outside the box!

Our instincts inspire us to look beyond the usual and identify the unusual. If we're attuned, our instincts transfer principles from one field of study to another, mix metaphors that yield new insights, and create fresh designs from tired traditions. Our instincts identify relationships among disparate people, places, and principles before we do. They spot patterns, designs, and threads of commonality.

Bowerman saw a waffle iron and a tennis shoe and married them into a multibillion-dollar corporation! Just consider how many people had been exposed to the waffle iron and had seen tennis shoes but didn't have the instinct to merge the two concepts. Can you imagine going to the bank and saying, "I have an idea from a waffle iron that is going to make me rich"? There was no intelligence to support it. There was no data to refer to. The risk was built on an instinct that paid off with unprecedented success.

Once you have confidence in your instincts, you must never allow other people's refusal to believe, or their data to refute, what you instinctively know is true. Your instincts know the blueprint for success that's within you and how to bring it to life all around you. Don't give up or be deterred from your destiny just because it doesn't seem to fit a formula. As we say in Texas, "If you believe there's a fox in that hole, point your tail and keep on barking!"

CHAPTER 4

Out of the Cage

We've talked a lot about instincts so far in these pages, but what are they? How should we understand them?

At its core, an instinct is an inborn pattern of activity or tendency to act that's common to a given species. It is also a natural or an innate impulse or inclination. These instincts are not just the basic ones you might consider, such as for survival, procreation, or fight-or-flight situations.

In my research, I was surprised to discover that some experts believe many people possess an instinct or a natural aptitude for making money, others for healing, creating art, organizing, or negotiating. I'm convinced our instincts emerge out of and alongside our gifting, so it makes sense that our instincts would reflect our talents and abilities.

As one expert from Psychology Wiki explains, "Any behavior is instinctive if it is performed without being based upon prior experience (that is, in the absence of learning), and is therefore an expression of innate biological factors. Sea turtles, newly hatched on a beach, will automatically move toward the ocean.... A joey climbs into its mother's pouch upon being born. Honeybees communicate by dancing in the direction of a food source without formal instruction."

Roar of the Entrepreneur

Regardless of our particular instincts, they all share a common direction: forward. Going out into the wild frontier of possibilities means you have to wean yourself from the nurturing state of normal and accepted practices. All of life is available to us, but not everyone will go through what it takes to enlarge our lives and reshape our environment so that we can release our instincts.

Visit your local zoo, and there you will see animals

living in cages. As long as the animal—say, a lion—stays in the cage, he knows exactly when he will eat. Cages are comfortable. Cages are consistent. They provide security. And generally they are safe. And yet I suspect there's often an alluring urge within our golden-maned friend in a cage to see what's beyond the safety of his warm bed and conveniently placed water trough in the cage's corner.

For the animal born in captivity, there's no basis for comparison. His needs are met and he is safe. "Isn't that enough?" many may ask. But if the cage were truly natural, then why must it remain locked? Keepers lock cages because animals are instinctively drawn to the wild, even if they have never lived in the wilderness. The lion longs for something he may never have experienced, even when his needs are met in the cage.

This is the roar of the entrepreneur. It's not that she can't get a job and be safe. It is that she is attracted to the frontier beyond the cage. The comfort of present limitations may be safe, but where there's nothing ventured, there's of course nothing gained. Most creative innovators eventually migrate from the familiar cage of controlled environments into the wild and, yes, dangerous frontier of entrepreneurship.

Whatever tickles your instincts, it will be something powerful and persistent. Regardless of where your instincts may lead, the question remains the same: Do you have the courage to adapt to the wild after living in the cage? Or, to put it another way, what do you do when your experiences conflict with your instincts? What if you're raised in the ghetto but have instincts for the suburbs? It's the lion's dilemma. If you were trained for a job but have the longing to be an entrepreneur, you feel his pain. If you long to be in a loving, stable relationship but have known only breakups and heartbreak, then you see through the lion's eyes.

The jungle beckons but the cage comforts. Our future awaits but our present is powerful. Thus, we struggle to connect with our calling.

Even after the decision to take the risk has been made, the fight is far from over. In many ways, it's just begun. If for some reason this animal, which was never created to be caged but has been all of his life, is placed in his natural habitat—the jungle that he was always meant to be in—he may die.

Although his instincts still reside within and will eventually surface, this transition into the wild may be difficult or fatal if his natural instincts are not reawakened and gradually restored. Leaving a cage for the opportunity to discover the freedom of your true identity requires not only leaving the safety behind bars but also learning to harness the wilderness within.

What is natural may not feel normal, because your experiences don't match your inclinations. Just because something is natural doesn't mean it feels normal when you have never had an opportunity to explore the true essence of your instincts.

Cages and Stages

Imagine how important it is that we wean the lion from the cycles of the cage and gradually reintroduce him to the primal sensation of freedom. That alluring gaze at freedom from a structured job or career may tantalize you with the notion of being your own boss. But I must warn you that the sensual notion of freedom can be a seductive trap if you don't understand that you are stepping into a world that isn't as carefree as it looks.

New predators, new diets, and new abodes await you. You will have to learn to hunt your own prey and avoid being someone else's. Although many of us aren't happy in cages and feel drawn to the wild, we must never underestimate the fierceness of freedom and the danger of the new world of self-fulfillment.

Instinctively successful individuals almost always have had to go through a metamorphosis in order to free themselves from their cage-like habits. And more important, they need time and training to adapt and to develop the instincts that are critical to survive in the new environment. If the lion needs that adaptation space to develop a more natural instinct, we, too, have to be prepared to be mentored and tutored even when we possess the instinct to increase.

The unborn baby lies in a cage we call a womb. He has eyes but cannot use them, and a mouth that he has never eaten with. He has been innately equipped for a world he has not been exposed to. His innate instincts like sucking, seeing, walking, and sitting have never been utilized because no opportunity exists in his present safe and warm cocoon of development. He must be born and enter the world to discover the instincts imbued by his Creator.

Cages and wombs come in all kinds of shapes and sizes. It doesn't have to be a dead-end job to be a cage. It can be renting as opposed to owning a home. For some it is the desperate clinging to singleness for fear of the heart-racing perils of intimate partnership. Many would rather sit at a table for one than risk the awkwardness of bolting into the uncertainty of coupling. In that new cycle of circumstances the cost of admission is the risk of rejection and abandonment. We all have cages of comfort that protect us but also isolate us from discovering not only what lies outside but also what lies within.

The baby cannot grow and mature into a healthy child until he leaves the womb. He is finally birthed into something bigger, and it is only after the cord is cut that he discovers within himself unused instruments that have only just become activated. I fully believe that many people never really leave the wombs of simple survival to venture into the bigger world beyond.

Now, you must understand that birthing is traumatic. Over and over we repeat the process. We go from the womb to the family, which is also a controlled environment that feeds and sustains us. By the time we adapt to our family, we are birthed into the world around us, and we have to activate instincts of survival or return to the cage of living at home again!

The Hell of Regret

He who wins the race cannot run with the pack. And once you get out, you can't come back, because caged lions don't mate with free ones! If ever you are going to win, you must forsake the social construct of the cage and all the cage dwellers. Whether they are business associates, community activists, political pundits, or any other order that has spoken and unspoken rules, you will have to take your own stand. This is never easy.

I cannot tell you how many times I have been that animal who hears the sound of the gate creaking open and momentarily freezes in place. And then, with a racing heart, I step into a world where the first terrifying sound I hear is the same gate closing shut behind me. So many times I have not known the lay of the land I was about to explore, but I knew that the passage behind me had closed forever.

This rattles the nerves. And yet, we must consider facing our fears and asking what we will regret the most. I'm not as afraid of dying as many people. I learned early that death is a part of life. My greatest fear is not living before I die—to play everything so safe that even though I had no risk, I also enjoyed no reward.

You see, the Olympic race of fear within you has but two contenders. One is the claustrophobic fear of staying, and the other contestant is the heart-pounding, adrenaline-releasing fear of stepping into the unknown world before you. This race is especially close when instincts take you where your history forsakes you. And there you are left alone with the frightening prospects of that which feels foreign and yet entices the instincts within.

I am afraid of spending my whole life with the deceptive deduction that my cage is the world! So when death tolls and life's final buzzer shrilly ends my tournament, more tragic than the end of the temporal would be the eternal hypotheticals of "What if...?" When I consider such a fate, the hell of regret singes my soul. The agonizing anguish of wondering what I might've been or done if I'd had the courage to free myself from learned behaviors and the cages life imposes is indeed the wind beneath my wings!

I'm not talking about just the cages of calling and careers but something much more significant: the cage

of contained thought. The sanctity of the orthodox, suc-
cumbing to living in the land of the average, seems a
massive waste of will and wit.

I faced this very dilemma when I made the decision
to move my family and ministry from Charleston, West
Virginia, where I'd grown up and lived all my life, to
Dallas, Texas, which I probably knew better from television and movies than from my own experience. I'm
still not exactly sure how it came about. I became inter-
ested in the Dallas area because I had heard that many
people there attended church regularly (not always the
case in urban areas) and were open to joining a new
Christian community. I had also heard that property
was relatively affordable for such a large urban area.

Ironically enough, I had actually told a friend of
mine, another pastor, that he ought to move to Dallas and start a church there. But after some thought-
ful and prayerful consideration, he ended up going in
another direction. And yet the thought of this place
I had recommended to him haunted me. I began to
wonder what Dallas was really like. While I had been
through there a time or two, I knew very little about
the people, the culture, the flavor, and the lifestyles of
Texans. And yet I couldn't quit thinking about moving

to the Dallas–Fort Worth area. It remained an alluring attraction, one I finally could not ignore.

When I went to Dallas and visited the prospective property for a new church, I asked the owner if I could have a few minutes alone in the building, and he agreed. There in the echoing cavern of a structure so much larger than our entire church back in West Virginia, I asked God if this was where he wanted me. It didn't take long before my awareness of his presence increased and everything in me heard "Yes."

Even with this sense of God's calling and blessing upon the move, I remained fearful. I had lived in West Virginia my entire life! I would not only be leaving my church to plant a new one, but I would be leaving one lifestyle and culture for another. The Dallas–Fort Worth metropolitan area included over two million people at that time—about twenty times more than Charleston! And how would Texans take to an African American outsider moving into their territory? If everything is bigger in Texas, would that include prejudice and hostility?

With growing trepidation, I agonized over this decision. I paced the cage that contained me and wondered if I dared set foot into the Texan jungle opening before me. If I stayed put, would I regret not exploring this opportunity, forever wondering, *What if...?* Or would I long for the comfortable security of my humble roots and regret taking the risk when inevitably confronted with adversity?

Moving away would include uprooting my wife and kids and taking my mother with us after she had lived over six decades in the same area. We would be leaving the small-town warmth of our cocooned community and launching out on new wings. But would we fly? Or flutter momentarily before crashing to the ground?

It was a huge risk, but I had to take it. I had to leave my cage in order to confirm my calling.

Not only did I feel God's prompting to make the move, but something deep inside me knew it was where I belonged— even if I didn't exactly know why. Needless to say, I have never regretted my decision to follow my instincts and move to Dallas. No, instead I discovered that my move was not just an open door to me but was in fact the intersection of the destiny of thousands if not millions of others whose lives would forever be changed, all predicated upon me releasing my fear and mustering the courage to be stretched beyond my comfort.

CHAPTER 5

Surviving a Stumble

Once you've overcome some of your fears and left the cage, you must keep moving. Once you've conquered certain limitations, you never stop. The dreams may get bigger, the challenges more daunting, the opportunities more thrilling, but your journey into the wild never ends. Once you've mastered the new wild, it eventually seems too domestic. It gives way to new opportunities and the next wild is always before you.

However, sometimes the key to following your instincts to the next level of success is all in the timing. It's not only a matter of when you jump but your pace as you transition to the next new jungle. Sometimes we must stroll out of the cage gradually rather than jump into the jungle suddenly.

When trainers introduce domesticated lions back into the wild, they do so in incremental steps. The lions leave their cages and spend time in their natural habitat before returning to the cages, then venture out for a longer duration on their next excursion with the trainers. Eventually they remain in the wild and never return to the domesticated home that once enclosed them.

This model works equally as well and is obviously more cautious and perhaps more practical for many people wanting to follow their instincts out of the cage. Please understand that I do not advocate taking foolish risks and closing doors and burning bridges without some semblance of support from which to draw your sustenance. It's one thing to take a huge risk, but it's another thing to live in the jungle on the first day!

So sometimes we stroll out of our cage, explore the terrain, return to our cage for a while, explore the jungle again, and so on until we can navigate the wilderness and forge some semblance of a way forward. To put it another way, we must look ahead and anticipate what we can handle. Scripture tells us that we must count the cost before we build our house, and the same is true with leaving the cage. If you know you don't have resources to support you for the first year and beyond, then don't quit your job to explore the jungle of your instinctive passion. Instead, start a side business or take a class; find a mentor or volunteer in an organization centered on your interests.

This is a safer model for leaving your cage and it balances the external realities of your responsibilities with the relentless longing of your internal instincts. When you take baby steps, you discover the strength of your legs before you try to run. You're still on a high wire, but there's a safety net if you fall.

Instinct May Initiate Failure

As you leave the cage, the transition into the jungle will definitely be challenging. You take a few steps forward and a few back. You stumble and fall and get back on your feet. Such is the way we learn to lean forward and keep stumbling toward success. For the newborn baby as well as for a first-time mother, those first attempts at nursing can end in painful disappointment. The baby has to learn how to receive nourishment from the nipple when it is offered. The mother has to learn patience and stamina as she passes the nutrients of her milk to her child.

In other words, it is totally normal to struggle as you leave the cage and acclimate to the new wilderness before you. Toddlers typically stumble, bumble, and trip before learning to walk. But they keep getting back on their feet and tottering forward until they no longer have to think about keeping their balance. Similarly, when learning to ride a bicycle, whether as a child or an adult, one is bound to lose control and crash until the complexity of simultaneous skills becomes second nature.

Many people do not get admitted to college, pass the bar, or become licensed in their field until after several failed attempts. But they persevere, undeterred, wiser and more committed to achieving their goal than they were during the previous attempt. My mama always said, "The world is our university and everyone you encounter is your teacher. When you wake up each day, make sure you go to school!"

It's not how many times you have failed; it's what you've learned each time you got back on your feet. Did losing that job a few years ago help you discover the kind of work environment where you can thrive? Did auditioning for that role you didn't get make you more determined to practice harder the next time? Did declaring bankruptcy for your home business enable you to manage your finances better for your new company? Each time you fail, there's a clue to your future success.

We need to fail boldly if we want to succeed extravagantly! So often successful people do not reveal their failures—and why should they? We cannot fault them for not wanting to make their mistakes front and center, especially when they have clearly overcome those obstacles to reach the summits of their particular mountains. But we must remember that the person whizzing by you as you struggle to keep pedaling has just as many skinned knees as you do!

Successful people follow their instincts beyond the emotions of their failures. They keep their eyes locked on the future even when they stumble in the present. That's how they keep moving in the direction of their destiny.

Instincts Transform Failures

Let me share one of the most educational experiences of my life—or, to put it another way, one of my most spectacular flops! Early in my career as a pastor, I decided to stage a production of my Gospel play based on my book *Woman, Thou Art Loosed!* and take it on tour. Talk about a comedy of errors! Just about everything that could go wrong *did* go wrong!

I was trying to preach at the same time the show was going up, dividing my attention and keeping me stressed onstage and in the pulpit. Rehearsals were disastrous, and the blocking seemed clumsy and awkward. Ticket sales were so poor that we had to give away a large number at the last minute to fill the auditoriums we'd booked. I soon realized I had hired the wrong people and ended up having to fire some of them the same week we opened.

There was simply so much I did not know about how to open a show and take it on the road. I didn't know that you open it in small markets to work out the kinks before taking it into large cities. I had no clue how to effectively market and promote this kind of dramatic endeavor. I didn't know which people to hire and which to avoid, or which venues were better than others and which to avoid altogether because they'd scalp you!

This experience presented a great opportunity to give up. I had invested my own money in it and couldn't afford to keep it going for long. I couldn't afford to ascend the steep learning curve that continued to loom before me. And yet...I couldn't afford to quit. I loved seeing a story inside my imagination come to life on the stage. I felt compelled to share a message with an audience hungry for hope. It wasn't just the financial and emotional investment in the show; it was the investment in my future I could not afford to give up.

So I knew I had to find a way to keep going, one way or another. You've heard the saying "Fake it till you make it"? Well, I "faithed" it till I made it! I learned the hard way how to make cast changes at the last minute and how to market plays and sell tickets so that the cast could get paid. I learned about lighting, music, theater acoustics, and the difference between amateur and professional actors.

I also met a young playwright and actor named Tyler Perry who was touring with a play of his own, *I Know I've Been Changed*. After being so amazed at his dexterity with language, storytelling, and acting, I requested a meeting with him and asked him to help me with the script for my own play. He graciously agreed, and we formed a friendship and professional relationship that continues to this day.

Through working with Tyler, I realized that often when you're laboring to come out of the cage, you must follow someone who's already a few paces ahead of you. These other risk takers already know where to find water, where to look for food, and whom to avoid in the jungle. They will often help you if you ask and allow them to impart the wisdom they've acquired in the wild.

As you can see, I learned so much from that string of painful mistakes and frustrating miscues. Should I have quit after that first disastrous run? Probably! But could I quit? No, my instincts wouldn't allow it.

And for good reason. I could never have imagined that now, over three decades later, I would be making films, consulting on scripts, casting, filming locations, and budgets. The exhilaration I felt at the premiere of my first major movie, *Woman, Thou Art Loosed*, could never have occurred if I had given up. If I had followed logic, I would have lost so much more than the education that can only come from mistakes and the school of hard knocks. Following my instincts, even through what felt like the valley of the shadow but was actually just a new jungle, led me to the fulfillment of my gifts.

All Eyes on You

I'll never forget being on safari and sitting out under the night sky with thousands of diamondlike stars glistening brightly above us. Since there were no artificial lighting sources—no streetlights, skyscrapers, billboards, or shopping malls—the dark seemed thicker and deeper, which only made the starlight seem brighter.

There were faint sounds occasionally from the bush surrounding us, but overall it felt peaceful and relatively quiet. That is, until our guide shone his flashlight in a 360-degree sweep around our campsite! As his beam penetrated the surrounding foliage of the African bush, dozens of luminescent eyes glared back at us. It's one thing to know those creatures are out there, but I'm telling you, it's another to have them staring back at you! They were watching us, scrutinizing our every move, prepared to fight or flee, depending on our actions.

Once you leave your cage, you, too, will be watched and scrutinized by dozens of people. As you become uncaged and integrated into your latest jungle, there will be plenty of naysayers, critics, and skeptics. But keep in mind that, like the eyes shining back at us on my safari, most of them will not physically hurt you. They may frighten you and make a lot of noise and increase your anxiety, but ultimately you must ignore their stares and remain focused on creating your own path.

Once you enter the jungle of your new endeavor, some people will be jealous, while others will feel threatened or intimidated. Some will want to compete and compare, and others will try to cover and capture. In the midst of such adversity, you must sidestep the dangers they present and follow your own instincts.

When others offer advice, criticism, or instruction, you should listen, consider it, and keep it in mind. But ultimately you can only follow your own instincts and not someone else's. Steve Jobs was right: you must never live anyone else's life but your own. You must fly on your own two wings!

CHAPTER 6

Finding Your Bearings

We've seen that your God-given instincts are key to unlocking your divinely appointed potential. To connecting with your calling and powerfully living out your purpose.

But relying on your instincts alone is not enough. You might survive but you won't thrive without due diligence and the research needed to sharpen and hone your instincts. I'm convinced instincts operate most accurately when they have as much data as possible. Our instincts then process the facts, figures, and financials through the filters of our personalities, experiences, and goals. It's where art and science meet to create this most unique navigational system for living.

As we learn to live by instinct, we will draw on all we've experienced: all our tests and tragedies, triumphs and setbacks. Curiously enough, the word *science* is derived from the Latin word *scientia*, which at its core means "knowledge." And knowledge comes in part from experiences and in part from encounters.

Every systematic enterprise must build and organize acquired knowledge in the form of testable hypotheses and calculated predictions about its environment. Before making assumptions based on prior knowledge, compare what you've learned to what you observe around you. If you study your strides, you're less likely to stumble!

Know Your Boundaries

While it's wonderful to know what you know, wisdom requires that you also know what you don't know without getting the two confused. There's much to be learned about where you are and how what you know fits into what you do not know. When the technician ascends to management, she must quickly recognize that people require more than mechanisms. When the employee becomes the employer, he must resist hiring and firing based on where he used to be instead of where he is.

Several years ago, during an election year, I was invited to the Christian Coalition of America because I was an up-and-coming minister whose biblical views might have made me a good prospect for the right wing. And that same year I was asked to speak at the Rainbow Coalition! Its members recognized that there were many issues that the coalition cared about that deeply concerned me also.

Both groups had invited me in part because of my growth in ministry and my arrival on the shores of this new world of public policy and political activism. As I went to both meetings and listened and watched and prayed, I knew that I had stumbled into a big field of ideas and dangers, secrets and sciences, that I would spend the next few years trying to untangle. And in the midst of all the push-pulling of my new peers, the operative question in my mind reflected the query of any new immigrant: Where do I fit, if at all, in this new and exciting world?

Now, you might say, "I'm not Bishop Jakes and I don't have those issues to balance and sort through." But before you draw this conclusion, think again. Whether you're a new hire, a new business owner, a new partner in the club, a new investor in the firm, or a newlywed, this applies to you. If you're a new alto in the choir or a new council member in the city, you have stepped into a field filled with fire and folly. Don't think for one minute that you can pretend to be unaffected by the forces flying at you from every direction!

Don't assume that you can rely on your instincts for information that's easily accessible in other ways. In other words, know the facts before you reflect on your feelings. Do the work necessary to be up to speed and informed about all angles of a problem, conflict, or issue.

I would like to think that I've been able to serve presidents and other political leaders in both major parties because of my ability to understand where they're each coming from. Although I may not agree with certain stands, statutes, or strategies, I try to respect others by seeing things through their eyes.

In other words, your instincts need to know the boundaries before they can help you get your bearings. Just as animals mark their territory so that they will recognize it later, we need to know the lay of the land before we begin traipsing through it. Is that the North

Star or a train coming toward us? Is this snowball going to roll until it causes an avalanche or will it melt at our feet? Without tending to the basics of investigation and research, it's impossible for our instincts to guide us accurately.

Heightened Instincts

Now, you can read the employee manual or Google the data on your new venture. You can gather the statistics and memorize the demographics in your mind. But the truth remains that in each new jungle you enter, an unwritten code of conduct guides its inhabitants. Each world has a host of special interest groups, causes to join, fraternities and sororities, and secret societies. These various groups will be blazing trails to mark their territory while you're still using GPS to get across the street!

Remember that while you're the immigrant learning the lingo, everyone else is native to the process. So before you take a nap under a tree or make camp in a clearing, you'd better poke around the bushes and discern what else is lurking around you.

There are ways to get things done that aren't recorded. There are ways to inherit enemies, encounter bullies, and sabotage your success that you haven't even thought about. And there are thousands of predators right in your own backyard who don't come out till the sun goes down. You might not see these night stalkers, but wherever you go, the gang's always there!

Balancing who you are with where you are is another science all to itself. On one hand, if you do not define yourself, your enemies will try to define you. So you have to be busy in the business of branding. But while you're trying to get the right message out about who you are, you must also learn to locate yourself within the context of currents swirling around you. Variable conditions, allegiances, and allies shift frequently. If it weren't enough to adjust to the new world to which you're acclimating, you must also become adept at negotiating negatives and leveraging positives about what you came to do.

You'll barely have time to unpack your bags in Bugtussle, USA, before you're dancing with danger and waltzing with wolves. Strangely enough, your accomplishment cannot fully be celebrated before it's time to decamp, defend, and debrief. Whenever you're thrust into the wild, someone or something will immediately pick up your scent and make strategic decisions regarding their response to your arrival.

The agendas are endless, the enemies everywhere, and the allies often apathetic. Fan clubs and fight clubs all meet on the same street corner. The difference between a friend and a foe can be as subtle as the distinction between identical twins. That is to say, you can scarcely tell them apart! Anyone who has ever taken a position at a new company or married a pastor or moved into a new neighborhood ought to give me a good amen!

Finding Where You Belong

If you don't find a way to enhance your instinct through research, you forfeit the opportunity to belong. I've had to let many people go from my company and occasionally from my church staff. It wasn't always an indication that the person wasn't good at what they did. Many times the problem arose from their inability to acclimate to their new environment. They could do the task but could not socially and professionally adapt to new ways of interaction, communication, and delegation. It doesn't matter how good you are at what you do if you can't fit into your new environment.

It's a science, so study it. It's a laboratory experiment to discover what you can and cannot say. It's listening to your instincts as well as the insinuations of your new associates. And learning in the lab remains dangerous since not all chemicals mix well! Chemical reactions can produce powerful results that either destroy or create energy for the organization.

And keep in mind that scientists must get outside their laboratories. Like zoologists in the jungle, you must learn to study the creatures with whom you cohabit. You must dwell among them, but you can't be one of them. They'll let you know that you live on the same street but you might not be a part of the gang. Learning to survive with the gangs without wearing their colors to work is a tricky business. It is a process and, God knows, it is a science.

You'll realize fairly quickly that most species tend to stick together. The rabbits may scamper like squirrels, but they don't play with them. The coyotes are strong and quick, hungry and ruthless. They've learned how to join forces in a pack without inviting the bobcats or the jackals. Record the habits of those in your new jungle, but don't allow yourself to follow the same patterns unless you're making a deliberate choice.

Study Your Own Habits

The challenge is to accomplish your assignment without losing your identity. Your presence changes the ecosystem and alters the environment for better and/or for worse. In the process of adjustments there will be conflicts. There will always be those moments where principles you used in your former life disappoint you in your current environment.

This lesson is fundamental. You can't take everything you used before with you. Your ability to survive has everything to do with your ability to adapt.

Adapting and surviving requires that you know your own proclivities and preferences, your default settings and disciplines. You must protect your soft areas and use your strengths to provide cover. Increasing the power of your instincts means learning more about yourself than ever before.

Like all sciences, there will be failed experiments and

lost investments. But these will teach you something—through the power of elimination if by no other way—if you're willing to proceed patiently. The loss of time, effort, and dollars becomes the price to be paid when your ultimate objective is to accelerate and not just acclimate. When you want to reach solid conclusions and not tentative theories, then you must be willing to risk what you know for what you want to know.

Inform your instincts and you'll improve your potency, no matter what jungle you find yourself in!

CHAPTER 7

Joining a Tribe

Seeking out purpose and fulfillment may seem like a solitary exercise—something undertaken *by* you alone and *for* you alone. But don't be deceived. The potential positives of isolation are merely illusion.

Our instincts remind us that we are social creatures, made to be in relationship to others. You aren't meant to dwell alone. You're made to be in relationship for your own fulfillment and the enhancement of your ever-expanding community.

However, instead of maximizing the strength of our social bonds, we often allow social constructs and expectations to limit us. Whether these are imposed on us by society, our culture, our families, or our own perceptions and misperceptions, we frequently miss the mark of maximum impact and muddle through mediocrity! Too often, we limit ourselves and create barriers, visible and invisible, to opportunities around us.

But this is not how we were made! Like the lions of the field and the eagles of the air, we were born without the inhibition of constructs. Most animals dwell in groups, whether packs, prides, herds, flocks, or convocations. Yet the lions don't try to fly, nor do the eagles try to run through the wild!

We must stay true to our instincts. Our ultimate instinct is always freedom—freedom of thought, freedom of passion, and freedom of purpose. Too often we try to be what we are not! Soaring without limits is one thing, but we are the only species that has built fences and barriers, restrictions and walls. Man was the inventor of prisons, both literal and figurative!

You'll never fulfill your destiny until you break out of the constructs and move beyond the socially induced systems that define and limit what is within you.

Cast Your Net

Living successfully by instinct requires a variety of com
plementary talents and abilities working in harmony to
achieve results beyond what you could achieve by sheer
talent or hard work alone. You must build teams and
lead them instinctively toward the focused objectives
you've established.

But instinctive living will also extend beyond your
employees, coworkers, and casual acquaintances. Follow your instincts, and you will encounter people from
a wide spectrum of professional and personal endeavors.
Typically, we call this networking. And if you think
about it, nets are woven from strings going in different directions, tied together at points of connectivity.
Human nets must work the same way!

If you network only with people who do what you do
and have what you have, then there's no intersection of
variations. You might make a nice mop or wig, but you
won't have a net that benefits the world! Networks are
built on strands that cross lines and make connections in
spite of facing different directions or diverse perspectives.

Nets can capture, contain, and convey more than any

single string from which they're woven. Fishing with a single line may be fun, but it is always a slow process. More times than not, Jesus used people who handled a net and not a line. There's a benefit in working with a net that a single line can never touch: the potential to increase effectiveness by diverse associations.

As an instinctively creative person, sooner or later you will come up with an innovative idea that exceeds the parameters of where you've been before. You start out trying to accomplish something that is within your scope, and soon you are beyond the borders of your territory.

During this journey of forging new partnerships and wrangling new relationships, I want to share with you the tools you need to go beyond the known maps of the past. These four basic principles will help you manage the opportunities that exceed the boundaries that you or others have placed on you.

Instincts Inspire

First, you must consider your inspiration. If you have something on the inside that instinctively inspires you beyond those around you, this will help you understand why you don't fit. People who are meant to lead have trouble being satisfied with those who seek the normal and are satisfied with the status quo. Their inspirations instinctively take them beyond barriers and lead them to color outside the lines.

Inspiration springs from an instinct, an internal compass that points across familiar lines toward the unknown. Like a spark igniting tinder into a flame, inspiration ignites you to act on what you envision in your imagination. Others may encounter the same external stimuli but fail to have it inspire them with new ideas or innovative approaches. Those who balance their intellect with instinct know that inspiration is often their offspring.

Your mind takes in data, performs due diligence, and processes information. But your instinct converts knowledge to power. Your instinctive deductive reasoning becomes inspired. It guides your quest to move beyond the scope of those accomplishments of ordinary people and will likely require you to blaze trails and cut through fences.

Inspiration is such a powerful tool and explains some of the way our intelligence complements our instincts. We take in information as raw material, as fuel, and then our instincts shape it into the best form for our current needs. This ability to adapt what we know externally with what we know internally yields the inspiration to bridge the two.

Whether we call it a hunch, an intuition, or a crazy idea, inspiration creates a fire that can provide heat, warmth, and energy in a situation that would otherwise remain cold and flat.

Instincts Intersect

This artful arrangement of alliances forms our second major tool, which I call intersections. Finding the inter-section points among diverse associations provides the key to maximizing the opportunities God has given you. Like a driver who wants to reach a certain des-tination, you can't arrive there without making some turns at crucial intersections. On the highway, we find an intersection when an east-to-west road crosses a north-to-south road. Two routes running in different directions briefly meet and cross at this point of mutual contact. Neither road changes directions, but travelers benefit from this connection because it enables them to reach new destinations.

When you follow your instincts, you will find yourself at the intersection of needing to build alliances with people who complete you rather than people who compete with you. Completion occurs when you join forces with others who may not be going your way but whose vision joins with yours to find an intersection. In this way, the relationship is built on what connects you rather than alienates or divides you.

Find the touch points of what you have in common with people, and don't be so inclined to focus on what divides you. Again, you can't make a turn until you find the corner. This place of connection is what I'm calling the intersection of ideas and inspiration. If we build on what unites us rather than focusing on what divides us—whether in a family, a church, or a business—we can achieve amazing goals with unlikely people because we understand the power of an intersection.

This process is the same no matter the scale or number of participants. Government and church intersect at the place of human needs. Business and philanthropy have different goals until they recognize the benefits of collaboration; big business needs a tax benefit and not-for-profits need funding. Suddenly their interests intersect. But if they only focused on the major differences between them, then they would both lose out on mutually beneficial opportunities.

You will miss these kinds of benefits if you forge alliances only with those who do what you do.

Instincts Integrate

Now, once we've found the intersection of common needs, we must look for the proverbial win-win, a convergent strategy encompassing the desired outcomes of all stakeholders, which I call integration. Whether in business, marriage, or other areas of life, alliances work only when both parties' needs are met and respected in a cross section of opportunity.

An integration of expectations is the goal we want to pursue.

In this pursuit, the art of negotiation becomes an essential tool. You don't have to be Warren Buffett to need to understand the power of negotiation. Those who negotiate from a selfish perspective of getting what they want at any cost, without integrating a plan that includes and respects others' needs, will always fail. An integrated strategy inherently addresses each individual party's motives, agendas, and goals in the midst of their larger, shared goal. This integration-based strategy includes the fulfillment of those needs in such a way that all differences are respected without losing sight of the ultimate objective.

Also, allow me to explain the crucial difference between merely tolerating these differences versus integrating them. The term "tolerance" is, in my view, deeply overrated. Tolerating differences might be an expression of political correctness, but in order for people to feel fulfilled in life, they must be much more than tolerated. They must feel that their talents, resources, and needs are an integral part of the planning. No one feels comfortable when they're merely tolerated. Toleration tends to be a temporary token. Most people can tolerate for only so long before their patience wears thin and shreds the garment of acceptance they gave to others.

If you want to be successful and outrun and outthink the herd, then you must negotiate by respecting differences and accommodating them in such a way that people feel that their uniqueness isn't just tolerated but is respectfully integrated into the plan. Women in the corporate world appreciate employers who include paid maternity leave and child care. Such benefits will not be used by all, but their inclusion indicates an awareness of personal needs that cannot be ignored. All employees, both female and male, respect employers who have an appreciation for cultivating and keeping the best talent in the company.

An integration of participants' needs and desires must be an essential part of any union in order for it to succeed. Including me without integrating what you know to be my needs as a spouse, a partner, a customer, an employee, or just a colleague ultimately dooms our relationship. If you're going to broaden your circle, you must change your thinking to integrate my objectives with your own. Without this component, the other individual, auxiliary, or company will only feel violated by the association, and the opportunity will eventually dissolve.

Instincts Execute

Finally, the fourth and perhaps most vital step is execution. A net doesn't work until it's thrown. No fisherman would make a net for fishing and leave it on the boat. You must know how to leverage your alliances by turning your integration strategy into action points.

Execution is critical for accomplishment. If you don't execute the plans you have in place, it doesn't matter how inspired you may be, it doesn't matter how meticulously you look for the common touch points of integration, and it doesn't even mean much if you integrate my needs into your plans. Inspiration without execution will always lead to frustration.

What needs to happen in order for this marketing campaign to have the major impact we want it to have for our product? Who's going to design the pop-up ads? Who's going to determine which sites they go on? Who's going to buy radio airtime? Who's going to make sure all the ads align with the same theme and consistent language? Who's going to follow up with consumer awareness groups? And on and on the process goes, until all the pieces are in place.

Your ability to transform inspiration into an intersection where integration takes place will only be as powerful as your execution. And eventually your ability to execute will become a matter of integrity. Are you known for having good ideas but not being able to follow through? For overpromising and underdelivering? Or will you be known as someone who not only follows your instincts for excellence but exchanges them for action and carries out decisions once you've made them? Especially with collaborative efforts, which we've seen are usually the most effective, it's an incredible breach of trust to other stakeholders when any individual does not do his or her part in the process. Everyone does their part in order to achieve the large-scale results that will benefit them all.

An instinct without execution is only a regret. As we've seen, all of us have the ability to achieve more by harnessing our intellect to our instincts. We need other people—more than just the usual suspects. Extend your net and make it work in new and instinctive ways. You might be surprised what you can catch!

CHAPTER 8

Welcome to the Jungles

The most frequent question I am asked when interviewed is "How do you manage so many different things at the same time?" When I try to explain, the best metaphor I can devise is that of a juggler. The art of juggling requires tossing two or more objects in a rhythmic sequence so that they continue moving without hitting the ground.

If you hold one object in your hand and toss it in the air, it's not really juggling. You're just tossing a ball. A juggler manages to keep objects airborne in a smooth, even flow that utilizes gravity in sync with his own dexterity. He keeps giving each object just enough of a push so that all items remain suspended and none falls out of sequence. If you hope to live by your instincts, then you must recognize that you will be a juggler.

How does this happen? Have you ever heard the saying "One thing leads to another"? This also holds true about the many worlds that you have to manage as you progress and take on new initiatives. Whether you are broadening your horizons or your current responsibilities are broadening you, life demands more to play every day! If you conquer one space, it creates opportunity and responsibility in other spaces and places. If you follow your instincts, not only does it open up the arena you're pursuing but it also expands your possibilities into other arenas you didn't originally anticipate.

Many people don't realize that instincts are not just a key to the next dimension; they're more like the master key that opens up new worlds beyond your wildest dreams. What feels enclosed by huge trees and massive shrubbery keeps going and opens up into an expanse leading to plains, rivers, and mountains. Every meadow is adjacent to another, so as you step into the one you expected, it will also be connected with others that you might not have anticipated.

Everything you touch is touching something connected to it. This connectivity is crucial to understand no matter what the field. Points of contact are used to measure the impact of marketing. Relational networks transmit the energy for global economics. Connections serve as catalysts for collaborations and corporations. Our technological connectivity has produced social networks that continue to cause some companies to rise and some to collapse. Opportunities, like the information highway itself, move at warp speed! If you understand the touch points, you can be far more effective than ever before.

Whole Wide World

If you have the kind of personality, product, or mission that excels, you will inevitably find yourself operating in several different jungles at the same time. The Bible says, "A man's gift will make room for him / And brings him before great men" (Prov. 18:16). If you follow your instincts and apply your intellect, your success will lead to new doorways of destiny and new windows of worldwide wonder.

In other words, a passionate pursuit of your purpose may lead not simply lead to *a* calling but to multiple callings. Multiple avenues for fulfillment.

From my experience and observation, this expansion of ideas and opportunities often occurs more frequently when you're focused on excellence in only one arena at first. People who take a shotgun approach and rush at everything available cannot maintain focus and gain enough momentum to succeed in any area. Ironically, when you deliberately try to take on multiple jungles, you may not learn to survive in any of them!

Growth isn't always a result of exceeding boundaries as much as it is shared interests and the common square of shared space. Consider the way business needs are interconnected and therefore conglomerates emerge. World markets ebb and flow and create economic tides that pour from one culture to another. Even in our shopping malls, retailers share common facilities to attract shared consumers.

The economics of the world are so interconnected that economic shifts in one country affect countries around the world. Now brokers have to be bilingual— or speak multiple languages—in order to be competitive, as their conversation is no longer communal but global. The brokers must be concerned about what's happening beyond their borders primarily because the borders touch. They don't just touch geographically but interculturally and relationally. So as they learn the language of the worlds they touch, they increase advancement and improve efficiency.

The message is clear: you can no longer stay in your lane and compete in the race!

Highly instinctive people have more to learn than the nuances of their home base. They must be astute at knowing more about the worlds they touch and how to understand the languages, cultural systems, and best business practices to meet those needs with proficiency and understanding. I can guarantee you, every action you make is touching more than who you think. You must realize that what you do in your corner affects the whole house, as we are all inextricably interconnected.

From One Jungle to the Next

Discovering the interconnectivity of your various jungles as you launch into new adventures of self-discovery will only enhance your journey. On a personal level, once you leave your cage, you are less likely to allow limits to define possibilities ever again. Beyond personal experience, you discover an overarching sense of purpose and destiny that guides you beyond your territory. Listening to your instincts gives you one of the best chances to make a real and meaningful difference in the world around you.

The ground you walk upon reverberates with the decisions you make and echoes with your lifestyle choices. Like anything that spreads by touch, instinctive influence cannot be contrived, controlled, or regulated. Your instincts will take you over the border and across the fence, and with them will come collaboration and cooperation. Once you have a sense of living by instinct, you will amass unlikely teams, connecting people, places, and things in a way others before you have never imagined.

Before long, your simultaneous environments will come together like spokes in a wheel that has you as its hub. And as your circle of contacts continues to enlarge, you will be able to cover more ground with each revolution.

But this is not about turning the wheel faster or winning a race; it's about your direction, your purpose. Connectivity must not be used to inflame the greedy or empower the selfish. It provides a guide to unearthing your power to function in a pluralistic society in various orbits for a purpose greater than yourself. It is this pursuit of your purpose and passions that lands you in a broader context, exploring new possibilities and challenging limitations. It is an awareness of the way fulfilling your own destiny allows others to fulfill theirs, both through example and through connection.

"And" Is More

As we learn to juggle, we often misperceive the bandwidth of our abilities. We mistakenly think we must eliminate or compromise one jungle in order to enter another. But here's the news flash: this isn't either-or!

Many times people choose what's next at the expense of forsaking what is. You could start a business *and* keep your career. You could explore your passion for music *and* start a family. You could remain on the corporate ladder *and* pursue completing your college degree. Not either-or but *and*!

It is possible to add without subtracting. If you add infrastructure to increase, you end up with empires that empower more than you can imagine! The idea of managing more intimidates some people, because they add by subtracting. Their way is to add this, take away that, and basically trade one for the other. They forget about creative, strategic moves that adapt to what's there and create more.

Your cup is supposed to run over. It not only overflows with abundance in your own life but into the lives of those around you. Your ability to juggle multiple worlds directly affects your community, producing new jobs, new ideas, and new universities.

Universities? Yes! Not necessarily the institutions of higher learning that typically come to mind, but a collection of people learning from one another. A university is simply a community of teachers and students, experts and apprentices working together—or, as it's expressed in Latin, *universitas magistrorum et scholarium*. The prevailing notion is that the up-and-comers learn from those ahead of them.

Learning from the masters prevents becoming enslaved! Most highly successful and accomplished people have mastered many worlds, which I'm calling "jungles" here. When we look to these people as role models, mentors, and teachers, we receive juggling lessons!

If you use this principle even on a small scale, it will bring order to your chaos and change the way you perceive obstacles on your path. More opportunity emerges when you organize a cluttered life. You can be philanthropic and profitable, work and volunteer, raise children and have a career, if you catch the principle. You can add to what you have without losing what you've accomplished— if you stop holding everything so tightly and simply learn to juggle!

Diversify Your Dreams

Your life should be as diverse as your interests. Think of the diversity exhibited in a shopping mall: one building with different stores but shared cost and leadership. A mall is the gathering of many stores around one common location. Look at what combined strengths do to marketing, management, security needs, customer traffic, and parking. A mall houses the seemingly unrelated under one roof and manages them all in spite of their diversity.

The one-roof concept unifies diversity. Finding the one roof, or the points of connectivity, is essential to bringing better management and faster movement to your life. Understanding what's touching the things you touch will help you move laterally and not take crazy leaps into wild choices. One of those points of connectivity in your world is you. You are the shared interest.

You are the ultimate brand. But there may be others, so keep looking.

In the case of the mall, we see many. They all need lights and heat, air-conditioning and maintenance. They all need management and, most important, they all need people. When you find what's common in your life, it lowers stress and organizes the future.

And you don't have to be the Galleria or the Mall of America to benefit from organizing the diverse interests into a structurally sound whole. Successful stores don't discard what brought them success even as they innovate for what's before them.

The demands on your life don't have to be identical to be interrelated. That passion you have, the vibrancy of your intellect, the experiences you've garnered, help propel you forward like a comet, grow into a planet, and soon become a new universe. This literally means that before long you are the tender and keeper of many fields.

Now is the time for you to build a team that enables you to better juggle the responsibilities and the opportunities that are waiting for you. What I want you to get from this chapter is how to touch everything you have, all the diverse areas of your life, from a position of maximized instinct.

CHAPTER 9

Aim High

Some time ago I was asked to be a guest journalist and contribute a series of op-eds for a prestigious media outlet. Despite my fears that my writing style and mental prowess could not compare with the impressive list of other contributors participating in the forum, I seized the opportunity and began to chronicle ideas. For my topic, I chose a fairly interesting but not controversial subject and addressed it with all the research and writing skill I could muster.

This was indeed a new forum for me, and, like most of us, whenever I step into a new arena, I want to do my very best work. So, before submitting my entry, I passed it around to a few of my brightest colleagues, who all pronounced it a stellar presentation worthy of that notable forum. Then, with a sense of confidence I hit the Send button, and a few milliseconds later, it was in the hands of the editor. She oohed and aahed about it in her response, and we started a process I really enjoyed…until I read the final copy!

Immediately upon publication, the online comments poured in and everyone had something to say. Some were contributing ideas and thoughts, others were complimentary and encouraging. But then I came to the rants and insults, and my heart sank into my shoes. I read post after post filled with such astonishingly acrimonious remarks.

Some of my negative responders attacked me as an individual, even though they actually don't know me and what I'm all about. Other critics attacked the topic of my article. A few didn't even seem related to what I had written; they just wanted to vent.

Needless to say, I was just floored. Shocked and appalled, yet still determined to penetrate the standards and earn the readers' respect, I wrote another article for the forum. The results were the same.

By the time I reached the deadline for my fourth contribution, I made some excuse for not contributing to the next edition and prepared to retire from the forum, assuming I was out of my league and over my head. However, a few weeks later I ran into the editor at a conference. She immediately asked, "Why have you stopped contributing to our forum?"

Shamefully, I said, "I got the impression I really didn't measure up to the standards of your readers."

"You're kidding!" she exclaimed in shock. "Why, your entries were some of our highest-rated ones!"

Now I was the one who was shocked. So I began to explain to her about the consistently negative comments I had received after each article. She actually laughed right in my face and said, "Those people aren't our audience! Our demographic is largely intellectuals who read for content and seldom comment other than to express another philosophical idea they deem significant enough to add to the dialogue. I seldom even read the comments after the article! Those shrill, angry voices don't want to be understood. They just want to make noise. They have nothing of substance to say!"

I laughed and walked away, disappointed with myself for allowing a few minor-league curveballs to knock me out of a major-league opportunity. Why did I allow "little" to remove me from "much"?

For quite some time, I couldn't explain why my sensitivity had assaulted my opportunity. It wasn't like me to be so easily intimidated.

But then I saw the giraffes.

Taste the Treetops

My defensive reaction remained a mystery until it came to mind during my safari. Watching a herd of giraffes illustrate a fundamentally instinctive principle, I found my answer from this surprising group of nature's towering tutors. Outside Johannesburg, across the South African plain, a galloping group of giraffes instructed me on what it means to eat at eye level.

From my guide, along with some online research, I learned giraffes are even-toed ungulates, the tallest mammals on earth. The males can reach heights of twenty feet, craning their six-to-seven-foot necks above their torsos. A stately species indeed, with their elongated necks, lithe bodies, and strong legs, they move gracefully and gingerly with an almost regal bearing. They struck me as the NBA team of the zoological kingdom, only with the movements of a ballerina as well as a basketball player.

I watched the giraffes stroll onto the plains like a float in a Thanksgiving Day parade, and it wasn't until they stopped to have an outdoor lunch that they taught me their powerful lesson. In spite of their long necks, which allow them to lower their heads almost to ground level, they didn't drop their heads but always ate from the tops of the trees. I was mesmerized.

I had never really considered how giraffes eat, assuming they grazed like other animals. But watching them stretch and munch mouthfuls of green leaves, I was struck by their own unique, up-in-the-air style. They clearly did not graze like many of the other creatures around their ankles. They liked the treetops.

And that's when I realized what I had done wrong in the situation with my forum. The small herd of magnificent mammals—their group is often called a "tower," fittingly enough—might as well have used a chalkboard to teach me their truth. Like the giraffe, I had aspired to new heights, but I couldn't keep my gaze at eye level because of the clamor around my feet. I had walked away from a twenty-foot opportunity because of the chatter I heard from two-foot thinkers!

I failed to realize that once you reach a certain level, you can't be offended by other species that look up from the ground! Once you get to a certain stature, you can't find nourishment in low places. Just because turtles dwell at your feet doesn't mean you should come down from your height and barter with, debate, or eat alongside them. As you rise, you must adjust your source of nourishment and affirmation accordingly. Yes, like the dinosaurs, there are times when you must adapt and bend your neck to eat—but only if there's no nourishment from the top!

When your influence and intellect evolve, you can't move forward without someone behind you criticizing your every move. Instead of eating a huge gourmet meal of the mud they were slinging, I learned to raise my eating habits to my sight line. I learned to always get a table on the top floor of thought and use a barometer commensurate with my own vision and goals to measure my efforts.

Feed What's Feeding You

Standing there beside the Jeep in South Africa, I kept my gaze focused on my new fascination, aware of what I was about to discover: giraffes were much more complicated than they appeared. It wasn't until my guide, the zoologist, began telling me about them that I realized how much I didn't know.

For instance, no one can deny the majestic beauty of the giraffe with its various shades of brown, a divine mosaic of chocolates and caramels painted by God himself. But as beautiful as the external view may be, the logistical diagram of its inner construction is where the mind staggers in sheer awe.

Its beautiful, curvaceous hide is a work of art when it moves. Beneath its artistic exterior is a richly well-thought-out biological masterpiece. The giraffe holds within its chest the largest heart of its species, a twenty-five-pound muscular pump capable of sending blood all the way up its massive neck to its head and brain.

Somehow the giraffe, by feeding from the tops of trees, nourishes this extraordinary heart. In its simplest form, the circulatory system forms a circle by which the body feeds itself.

You must always remember to feed what's feeding you; this cycle of nourishment is the source of our very survival. If it's a marriage, you have to feed it. If it's a business, you must pour resources back into it. If it's a church, a club, a friendship, an educational institution—whatever it is that stimulates you, gives you energy, and helps you be your best self—you must feed it in turn.

The heart of the car is the engine. It doesn't matter how the wheels glisten or how sophisticated the computer technology that operates its systems is. If there is no engine, nothing else is energized. The heart of the corporation is human resources. This is the department that hires and supports the right staff to fuel the vision of the CEO. If you don't build up your human resources, the company will eventually go code blue. You'll learn the hard way that talented, committed people really are your greatest resources.

The heart of the church is the Gospel. If the building is loaded with stained glass, great music, and social services but loses its core message of salvation, then it may be a great organization but it certainly isn't a church. For the brain to be sustained, the heart must produce a steady flow of lifeblood. The two must work together to move the body in synchronicity or you will never reach the heights for which you were created.

So ask yourself: What feeds your dream?

Heads and Hearts

At the heart of our instincts, we discover our primary purpose. Our purpose provides the message or mission by which we live out our gifts and talents. Our instinctive life mission cannot be purposeless and powerful. In film development, the heart of the movie is the script. If the screenplay doesn't feed the actor the lines she needs to develop a compelling character, then even the greatest actor becomes powerless to deliver the punch.

Have you ever seen someone have a heart attack? Their eyes go dim, their pulse stops, their mouth goes dry, and their pupils dilate. Why such reactions in the head when it's the heart that's malfunctioning? Obviously, the head along with the rest of the body manifests the effects of the heart shutting down. It is from the heart that the head and body have life.

The giraffe has a tongue like no other animal. It can reach around branches and pull down fruit, and its fur-covered horns are strong enough to ram through any obstacle in its path. However, none of its attributes and strengths matter without the heart energizing the activity. Yes, the heart must function properly to sustain the body.

Life sometimes presents us with strange teachers, but their lessons are often the most memorable. This has certainly been my experience with sighting a group of giraffes in the African bush. They immediately triggered an epiphany that allowed me to realize why I had let my loudest critics demotivate my budding journalistic efforts.

But more important, the giraffe inspired me to want to reach higher, extend my abilities farther, and taste new leaves. If you want to connect to your calling, feed your heart and stretch to the treetops!

CHAPTER 10

Act Now

I can still remember my friend the zoologist sharing with me how even the angles of certain animals' teeth were designed to gnaw at branches as a source of pruning so that both the food chain and cycle of life would not be broken. I thought to myself, *Look at how God has made all needs to coincide so that the animal's hunger serves as a gardening tool for the branches that provide his food!*

Relentless reliance on instinct not only supplies what we need but also becomes the vehicle by which all else around us is affected and sustained.

As we conclude, I hope your confidence is greater, your aim sharper, and your awareness of your innate abilities more finely honed. More fully immersed in the wellspring of your instincts, you will have an increased impact on the target before you. Whether you're aiming at a change in career or hoping to parent a child, I believe the answers we often seek from those around us are actually buried somewhere within us.

"As thy days, so shall thy strength be" (Deut. 33:25) literally means that in proportion to the demand, the resource emerges to fulfill the need. You have what you need when you need it! Maybe not always exactly when you want it, but when you need it.

Primal but Not Primitive

Once again, I want to be sure you understand that these concepts are not meant to give you any formula or template for success but to awaken what may be dormant or underutilized in your life. Sometimes recognizing the resources already available to us can be the most empowering moment of all. We are most effective when we draw from every God-given resource we have been given to survive in this world. Now, with the full armor of all that has been given to you, it's time to change the dynamics of the game.

We've had an exciting journey through concepts and precepts, jungles and junctures, as we've explored various nuances to seek purpose and fulfillment by using our instincts. However, all of it means nothing if we do not recognize that the investment of ideas merely prepares us for the opportunities with which we've been graced in our individual lives. If you believe as I do that we have been divinely pre-wired for a master purpose beyond ourselves, then you should be equally excited to realize that tapping into your instincts acknowledges your own unique purpose on this earth.

You see, our instincts not only exist to enhance our experience here on earth; they also provide evidence of a mastermind above us who placed all that we need within us. I believe that what God has given us is his gift to us. How we utilize what we've been given is our gift back to him. By shedding fresh light on something profoundly primal but not primitive within us, I've challenged you to consider new paradigms and empowered you to shatter the limitations of fear and frustration blocking your liberation.

Much of our attention has been invested into the introspective examination of bundling all that is within us to affect all that is around us. We now clearly understand that intellect without instinct is like a head without a heart. When we embrace all that is intellectual and psychological without including the deeply spiritual, the instinctive inclinations of our hearts limit us unnecessarily. Remember, Scripture tells us that out of the heart flow the issues of life—not out of the head!

You Have What It Takes

Recognize the adequacy of what is within you to survive and succeed amid all you face. You do have what it takes to master the outward challenges as you release your inner resources. But if you're going to accomplish this awakening of instinct within you, it's time to act. You must connect ideas to ideals and excitement to action. You must do more with this book than place it on a shelf or file it away in your electronic reading device.

Don't get me wrong. I love being able to share my ideas with you in these pages. Reading is the gymnasium of the mind. It is the place where thoughts are exercised and minds are stretched and challenged. However, through tranquility and deep reflection we are able to search the heart for answers that the mind alone doesn't contain. The mind may guide you in what to do, but the heart affirms your passion to do it. This is what will ultimately move you to motion.

Somewhere in your passions lie the clues to your deeper purpose. It is my hope that you will recognize the divine investment placed within you and garner all your resources to steward this treasure for the future before you. In short, you have what it takes! All that you need is within you and can be accessed instinctively. Understanding this truth secretes confidence, which I'm convinced has a lot to do with overcoming obstacles and releasing your inherent, resilient power.

So what is your deepest, truest message that you want to convey to the world? This is the moment when we need to clear our minds from the clutter and allow our instincts to guide the process of creative reasoning. If we can strengthen what is within us, we can change that which is around us.

I am excited to know that we are only one domino-toppling thought away from a cure for HIV-AIDS. I am excited that we are gaining ground on dread diseases like cancer, heart disease, Alzheimer's, and autism. Even at this very moment, the solutions to world poverty and global warming are locked in someone's mind and about to be unleashed by their instincts. Whoever holds the key to changing the world can't be someone who runs with the herd and fits in with the pack. Our world has always advanced through trailblazers who broke boundaries and shattered limitations.

Now I must confess, it is unlikely that any of these tasks are likely to be vanquished by someone like me. But that's okay. I will be happy to tackle the challenges within my view even if they gain no notoriety in the world of medicine nor instigate world peace. If my instincts do not lead me to a more perfect world and only succeed in granting me a more peaceful home, I will still be fulfilled.

If my instincts can aid me in my affairs and can be used to settle some of my problems as my life unfolds, then I will still be content. At the end of the day, I realize that all great people will not be famous. And all famous people will not be great. Instinct was never meant to ensure our recognition. Instinct may remain incognito but always inspires and initiates your success.

It propels us forward—but we need not all travel at the same speed. As we've seen, one of the gifts of our instinct is timing and knowing the pace of our current season. As long as we're moving forward, we will reach our destination.

About the Author

T. D. Jakes is one of the world's most revered communicators. He has been an adviser to three US presidents and has been called "America's Treasure" by Oprah Winfrey and "America's Best Preacher" by *TIME* magazine. Jakes founded the Potter's House, a nondenominational global church with more than thirty-thousand members and campuses around the United States. The Potter's House reaches tens of millions each year through television, radio, and the internet. He is also the founder of the T. D. Jakes Group, which is dedicated to solving society's problems by building bridges and strategic partnerships that create equity and provide solutions for underrepresented and underserved communities. Through partnerships and disruptive thinking, the T. D. Jakes Group continues to make connections across sectors and stakeholders to create lasting, generational change and a more equitable society. Jakes has more than forty best-selling books in print, including *Crushing*, *Instinct*, and *Don't Drop the Mic*. He has been a devoted husband to Serita Jakes for more than forty years, and the power couple has successfully raised five beautiful children.